Eco *and* Frendlee
Visit the Bog

Fulton Books
Meadville, PA

Published by Fulton Books 2024

ISBN 979-8-88982-552-4 (paperback)
ISBN 979-8-88982-682-8 (hardcover)
ISBN 979-8-88982-553-1 (digital)

Printed in the United States of America

Eco *and* Frendlee
Visit the Bog

L. C. Madalion

"I was waiting for you to get bigger.

You are bigger. However, you are still a puppy. I traveled around looking for a place to show you."

"I am bigger. So what do you want to show me?"

"Can you crawl under the fence?"

3

"Where are we going?"

"You'll see."

"Okay, let's go."

"When we go over this bridge, you'll begin to see where we are going."

"Wow, I can see it. What is that place?"

"Frendlee, it's a bog. It's also known as peatlands. The bog has dead plants which rot away slowly.

7

The bog helps keep the air clean and helps with climate change. The bog stores carbon dioxide (cleans the air)."

"Eco, the flowers are beautiful. What kind are they?"

"Frendlee, they are tiny iris-like flowers that open in the sunshine. Some of the plants are beautiful, some of the plants you can eat, and others are carnivorous. The word *carnivorous* means that they eat insects."

"Frendlee, don't chase the turtle. This bog turtle is classified as threatened and is on the endangered species list.

He is threatened by the lack of water [diminishing water] due to people building highways, other animals like raccoons and reptiles [snakes] who eat the bog turtle, and humans who collect turtles because this turtle is a rare turtle."

"Frendlee, the turtle is the smallest turtle in the world. The turtle has an orange patch on either side of its head."

"Eco, the turtle is so cute."

"Eco, I'm a little bit hungry. Can I eat this plant?"

"Frendlee, the frog is a true frog. It has a narrow waist and smooth skin."

"Eco, that kind of frogs legs are red."

"Frendlee, he is a true frog. The frog is three inches in length and has dark skin."

"Frendlee, don't chase the hare. He is a snowshoe hare because of his large-size hind feet."

"Yes, the snow hare has big feet."

"Eco, look at that thing with the orange teeth. What is he?"

"Frendlee, he is a beaver. His front teeth are orange because they get their color from the iron coating of their enamel.

This gives his teeth strength and prevents tooth decay. The beaver gnaws (chews) on wood to build his home."

"Frendlee, we have been wandering around the bog all day. It's late. We had better start for home."

"Frendlee, why are you looking back?"

"Eco, the best part of the day was the little turtle with the orange around his neck."

"Eco, I am going to crawl back under the fence. I am going to dream of where we will be going next."

References

Davies, Caleb. "Why bogs maybe the key to fighting climate change?" www.phys.org.

Florida Highwayman artists, who have been painting beautiful scene of nature. Copyright on May 15, 2023.

PEW Institute.

Proulx, Anne. *Fen, Bog and Swamp*. New York: Scribner, 2022.

www.education.nationalegographic.org.

www.wanderlust.co.uk. "Bogs are found around the world. However, some of them are disappearing. The bogs help with climate control."

Location of Bogs in the United States

Michigan
Wisconsin
North Carolina
New Hampshire
Kent, Ohio
Illinois
Maine
Virginia

About the Author

The author graduated from Neumann University (formerly named Our Lady of Angels) with a bachelor of arts in history and also attended Saint Joseph's University. She received a certificate in elementary education. The author graduated from Ball State University with a master of arts in counseling psychology and a certificate as an elementary counselor.

The author was impressed with the Florida Highwaymen's artwork. They are a group of black artists who have been provided America with beautiful scenes of our natural resources. This helped her decide to continue with writing about Eco and Frendlee and nature.

The author is a veteran of the United States Army. She lives in Lansdowne, Pennsylvania, with her collie, Redd Fox.